SECOND
TIME AROUND

BY

KYLIA JOHNSON

Second Time Around © 2022 by **Kylia Johnson.**

First Printing

ISBN# 978-1-955148-30-6 pbk

ISBN # 978-1-955148-29-0 ebk

A2ZBooks Publishing Lithonia, GA 30058 www.A2ZBooksPublishing. net. Manufactured in the United States of America A2Z Books Publishing has allowed this work to remain exactly as the author intended, verbatim.

To My Angel

We did it and although you cannot be physically here today to experience this, I know spiritually you are here and never truly apart. Thank you for raising me, believing in me, inspiring me, and most importantly loving me.

Miss and love you

Kyla

CONTENTS

Intro

I noticed second chances occur in the smallest form, not particularly considered do-overs, but opportunities that we take for granted and fail to see that we were given another chance. Sometimes we may spend a lot of time wishing, wanting, and dreaming about an opportunity when the opportunity is literally right there. The sad part is, you may never know you're not going to have that second time around with that very same opportunity again.

Every day of our lives, we are given chances that we don't usually take, but they're there for taking. I understand you may not know; I wasn't always aware either. Hopefully, by reading this book, you'll understand that every second counts and every chance matters. Every day you wake up, you're given a second chance to do whatever it is you want, be whoever it is you want so why not take it? Because truthfully, the only thing stopping you from being the best version of yourself is.... you!

Second Time Around Notes

Challenge your limit and never miss an opportunity. Ask yourself have you missed any opportunities?

_____

_____

_____

_____

_____

_____

_____

_____

_____

_____

_____

_____

Nine Lives

I was told a cat has nine lives. If that's true, then I know how a cat feels. The saying "you only got one life to live" truly is a saying we should live by. I never noticed until I was almost out of here that every second in life matters, especially if given another one. Here is a brief story about me and my upbringing. My grandma and my whole family are super religious. What's it called, a PK kid. Yea, I was definitely one of those.

While growing up, I was always told and taught about miracles, faith, and everything else you would find that was talked about in the bible. But hey, I was just a kid. I mean who had time to think about anything regarding church when Mario just a friend video just dropped. As a normal kid, I could care less, but I had no choice, so I did as I was told. So, back in middle school, I use to ride the bus. Oh, don't laugh because you did too and it was cool back then.

Nowadays, kids want to get dropped off in a helicopter – presidential style. Well, that one day changed it all. I was just being a normal kid, having fun with friends on the bus until it was time for me to alight from the bus. It was at that very moment that I believe was so unforgettable and it was something some people might call a miracle and with what I know now, it was most definitely my miracle. It's worth sharing because no matter what happened to me back then, somehow someone will be inspired or even blessed in some sort of way by reading this chapter and knowing that the miracles are real.

So on that day, I was getting off the bus and some reckless person blew through the big red STOP sign the bus pulls out every time they come to a stop which I'm sure we all should know means "stop kids are approaching." My friend Ramissee gets off first, and the bus stop was on her side of the block so I had to cross the street to get to my house. While I proceeded to cross the street, I heard my name and instantly, I stopped, took a step back and looked back to see who called me thinking it was just my friend.

It all happened so fast but within that same moment of hearing my name, an SUV truck came flying past disregarding the stop sign, and I mean on full speed. I felt the wind hit my face while the car continued to fly down the street. Turning around to hear my name being called, I looked and saw that Ramissee was already gone into the house, so it was impossible that she called me. I mean when I heard my name; though it was so clear and felt up close, I thought she was right there or at least still outside.

I looked at the bus driver thinking that maybe she called my name, but the window was completely shut, and no one else was around. As I stated before, everything happened so fast and all I knew was that in that split second, I had just missed death's door. With my size and height, I definitely would have been out of here. I knew it was unbelievable that in some way, this must be the miracle they talk about in church but I wasn't sure at the same time and probably didn't think anyone would even believe me.

Especially at my age, who would think I even knew what a miracle was. The bus driver put the bus in park, got off and watched me cross the street and told me while crossing "go get your mom." My aunt came out and the bus driver instantly said, "that girl is blessed, and it's a miracle that she's still alive." She went on to explain the situation and they continued to converse. I didn't really care about being so caught up in religion but that day, I was given a second chance at life.

I then believed that I was saved because of my background, the anointing I had over me and the prayers from different people covering my life daily. It's one of the reasons why I pray over my child's wellbeing at school or just on a regular day in general. Hoping that if anything ever happened to him – because truthfully you never know – that my prayers along with that of others may cover him. It may sound like a bunch of bs to some but in my opinion, I was able to experience a miracle, live life, and tell my story today from those same prayers.

I felt like I was given another chance to connect with my religion as well. When you understand my church methods, then you will realize why my family was so strong in living for God. I know everyone is different and won't have the same beliefs and values and that's okay. I'm not trying to change that. I'm only saying that in the smallest moment and at the youngest age, I was even given another chance.

"You have to take risks. We will only understand the miracle of life fully when we allow the unexpected to happen." **(Paulo Coelho)**

From that experience, I took another chance at understanding my religion and once I got older, I understood more. I could pick my own beliefs and express what I choose to believe in, but until then, learning mine was the better choice. Within the time frame of the incident, all I knew was that God had given me another opportunity to live, and I'm so thankful to be here to experience this life He's paved so far for me. At such a young age, I started to become firm and big on faith, grace, and hope.

On top of my situation, after all I experienced while growing up, I started seeing various people experiencing miracles right before my eyes. My grandma had cancer pretty bad but she lived much longer than doctors gave her. Every doctor she saw mentioned that it was a miracle for her to live for several months with her case of cancer – not even considering years after her diagnosis. My little cousin Asia wanted to attend Renaissance High School where you have to receive a letter of acceptance at that time to get in and she didn't get hers yet.

All the way up to the first day of school she still didn't receive one. She bought the uniforms and everything for that school year. She believed and wanted to only go to that school and we thought she was absolutely crazy. The first day of school came and she began to attend as if she was a student. She went to the office and as I write this today, my little cousin graduated with honors from Renaissance High School. Her faith was so mind-blowing and inspiring.

In high school, she really took the phrase "faith as big as a mustard seed" to a new level. She was going to attend that particular school without a letter because that's where she wanted to go and knew she had the credentials to attend. My older sister Tiera was involved in a terrible car accident several years ago and we thought she wasn't going to make it based on the reports we received. But today as a witness, my sister is absolutely fine, there wasn't any serious scarring or body parts taken away.

My sister is beyond blessed and we're glad she's still here with us today. In fact, she watches my son every Wednesday and that's a blessing itself lol. I know what you're thinking, "that's my family why believe me." So I'll share that of people I don't know. Based on a true story, the movie "breakthrough," what Joyce Smith and her family went through, experiencing that unbelievable miracle was so powerful, and if you haven't seen it, you're missing out. Truth be told, it happens to many people and even celebrities. Kevin Hart, Curtis, "50 cent," Jackson, Travis Barker, just to name a few, are all celebrities who I don't know personally but have all survived tragic car accidents, deadly shootings, and severe plane crashes while others ended up losing their life, realizing that miracles come in all forms.

Hearing about and actually seeing people just missing death's door like me, tends to remind me that God is real and with us all the time while miracles are still happening every day. I'm not also saying that you have to experience something tragic in order to witness a miracle. God's grace shows up in any situation, all day and every day. No one is saying you have to believe in God. By all means live your life because you may not understand or care but just be mindful.

I can only tell you my experience now because I was given a second time around to do so, and not too many people are that lucky. That one spring day changed my life forever. Hearing that voice, I realized it was God telling me to step back. Growing up, I'd always hear different prophets saying it was a calling on my life but I didn't know exactly what that meant. I did know then that if there was really a calling on my life, it was God saving me that day. Moving forward, I didn't know what he had planned for me, but I did figure it had to be something pretty special for Him to give me another chance at life.

Second Time Around Notes

Did you get a second chance at something? What did you do differently?

_____

_____

_____

_____

_____

_____

_____

_____

_____

_____

_____

_____

_____

_____

_____

_____

_____

11:11

Now, this is a section that at some point, was very hard to live through, and even more difficult to talk about. It was work in progress that I had to heal from mentally, and physically. It was a work in progress that I eventually overcame. Family is a very touchy subject and whether you like it or not, they are really not going anywhere unless God has another plan for them. Family is blood, and even though sometimes it sucks that we cannot choose to be born into the fantasy families that we sometimes tend to dream about, I'm sure at the end of the day we are extremely blessed to have the loved ones we have.

This is where it gets a little deep and difficult for me. Yes, my family irritates me at times, and I may get frustrated with them but overall, I love them to death even when I may not show them. With all the love I have for them at some point in life, I wished my mom wasn't my mom. Not because of having to follow simple rules, thinking life isn't fair, but because she was a drug addict and was in/out of my life. Instead of raising my siblings and me, she chose a way out of parenting by coping with drugs.

Unfortunately, I had the pleasure of witnessing both parents partake in that drug life, in/out of jail, and just basically living that street life. So, while growing up, they were not really there for me and my siblings, but my mom made the effort in coming back from time to time throughout the years. From what I remember up until she left, my mom was literally like my best friend. Being that young, I knew the love and fun spirit my mom was and it made her my favorite person.

I'd always have that feeling that no matter what, I could always count on my mom. Even now, she's still this "hilarious life of the party" person everyone loves to be around. My mom back then was so cool at least from what I remember, and it definitely was an adjustment not having that anymore. I wasn't at all prepared for all the pain and hurt my family and I endured from her absence. I just thought she could do no wrong at all – at least not to her children. Until I became a mom myself and realized that we're all human and that we will and we are going to make mistakes at some point in life.

Now, we don't always make the best decisions but it's not initially. I want to share my experience of giving my mom a second chance at rebirthing motherhood and just finding her way back in general from overcoming a strong addiction. A second time at forgiving, and not just saying it but actually feeling it in every way. Letting others who may have had absent parents – for whatever the reason may be that is keeping them from their responsibilities – know that there's hope, and I pray your situation gets better. It may not seem like it may ever will, but it will.

I pray that the situation and the trauma caused get restored and if not you as a person, I pray everyone will heal from it all. So, I have three blood siblings, my older brother Karl, sister Kandis, and then my younger brother Happy. My mom left us when I was about four. We were found in the house alone with both parents gone for a couple of days. My mom left us with a friend and went to hang out in the streets. My dad left months ago out of state trying to find something better for his family only to stay and not come back to get us, meaning that my parents were having problems already.

That left my grandparents to step in and take care of us until we could go back with my mom. Then it all became a bit too much for my grandma and grandpa. So Karl and Kandis were sent to live with other family members who wanted to help while Happy and I stayed together with our grandparents. It was bad enough not being able to live with my parents but also not being able to grow up in the same household with all my siblings was tough to tackle as well.

After having us for a few weeks, it wasn't funny anymore. So, my grandma called my mom numerous times to come get us, not knowing that it was the beginning of her addiction. My grandma thought my mom was just staying out late hanging with a bad group of friends and running away from her responsibilities. When she refused to make any progress in coming back to take care of her children, my grandma called the police just to scare her hoping it would make her come home.

Not thinking at all that when the police get involved in a situation, so do CPS at least when children are in the picture. Since it was considered neglect on my mom's end, we were brought in and taken away from my grandparents. Feeling so upset, my grandma tried to get us back but the state wouldn't allow it without a judge reviewing the case which resulted in not allowing us to physically move/stay with her at the moment. So, for about two to three weeks, while waiting, we were put in the system and placed in foster care.

My brother and I were devastated and got picked up by a woman who seemed to be in fostering just for the money. My grandparents would visit us regularly on visitation days, always checking in on us and making sure we were good. Until one day my grandma demanded we stay with her while waiting on paperwork. She received a phone call saying we were at the hospital due to a severe incident. Hot coffee was spilled on the left side of my little brother's face leaving him with burns.

After that incident, it was finally time and we were going home with our grandparents and officially adopted by them too. Extremely happy, it felt a lot better knowing we were safe, home and could count on them. My grandparents ended up being my whole world growing up. They gave me a sense of relief like a real homeness feeling with a lot of love. Occasionally, my mom would come by a couple of times in a month with money for us, without a clue how she made and got it.

I guess the reason why she was coming was to feel as if she was still in a way being a parent and making sure her kids were good money-wise. Also, to help my grandparents out when things got tight financially. I ended up hating her visits and loving them at the same time. The issue was seeing someone you love walk away, and not being able to go with them, having to wait until they come back or at least constantly think if they ever would. My grandma started to see the pain on our faces every time my mom left after a visit, so she insisted that my mom either got clean or she simply wasn't allowed to visit us anymore.

I'm pretty sure you have a good guess at which one she chose. It was a while before we saw our mom again. Even though we didn't see her much anymore, I still believed she would get clean and come back for us then later on maybe my dad. Although she was in the streets, she kept coming back to visit and drop off money, which at the time I thought had to at least mean something. My grandparents did their best and always wanted the best for us. A little later, my older sister came back to live with us because my grandma wanted to at least try and keep us all together and she also had help now.

My aunt and her family ended up stepping in and receiving guardianship over us, raising the three of us permanently from middle school and up with weekends belonging to my grandparents. It was like our bonus family with a two-parent household and more siblings, my cousins became my siblings. No matter how well we settled in and how happy we were with my aunt, we still constantly prayed for our mom to come home, like literally begging God to let her come clean and make up for lost time with us.

For a moment I knew God had heard our prayers, and for the first time since she left, my mom got clean and came back. We still lived with my aunt, but we were able to have visits from her when we went to our grandparent's house on the weekends. This was a great start and kind of looked as if things were going well for my siblings and me, at least that's what we thought. Then it happened, my mom stopped visiting or calling and ended up leaving us again. We first wondered if maybe something happened, but it became clear that she was back out there, on drugs, and on the streets.

After a while of crying wolf, it felt odd and very overwhelming to trust my mom time after time, Sushil Jakhar wrote *"Trust is like an eraser it gets smaller and smaller after every mistake."*

I knew it was just a sickness my mom was battling, and she still cared about us regardless. So, I continued to pray no matter how many times she messed up still having that small bit of faith. I prayed and prayed; I mean really prayed because this time if she went back out after being clean for months I would just finally give up. One promise I made to God; if my mom was able to get and stay clean this one last time, I figured I would show her all the love and support she needed. No judgment or being mad at her for lost time and moments but just do any and everything to keep her from going back out there again.

To at least help her realize what she was missing out on – the most important things in her life – that we were all she needed. Sooner or later, I learned it wasn't left up to us to make her realize but it was within herself. Just like that within a short time, things got magical for us. It was like a miracle; my mom really got cleaned up and turned her life around. She started working a nice job co-owning a building with a good friend, got her own car, and a little after that her own apartment.

I was thrilled and we all were so grateful for her getting herself together. I had my mom back and despite all she took us through, it didn't matter anymore because mommy was finally home for good this time. She started to make up for the lost time. I remember her taking us to hotels, trips downtown, just simple stuff I missed doing with her all those years. With everything going so well, it seemed my mom finally came to her senses and could do no wrong anymore.

After being clean for so long, a point came when we were completely crushed and devastated. Sad to say once again that my mom was leaning towards drugs. I give her credit because she lasted longer than the other times, but all that mattered was that it didn't last. One weekend my mom was supposed to pick us up, but she never came and never called. During the time she was clean, she bought my sister and me a little cell phone. I remember that weekend and days afterward just calling her and blowing up her line, leaving numerous messages because I felt she didn't leave us again. It had to be a mistake.

When my siblings and everyone else knew she was back on drugs once again but I just refused to believe it. It was not possible, after all, we were having so much fun. So I was not believing that at all. Then one day she finally called and I immediately asked a million questions hoping she would tell me what I wanted to hear and not what people were saying. But while she was trying to apologize to us, I could hear in her voice the guilt, the embarrassment, and shame. Tears just rolled down my face and it was the most striking pain I had ever witnessed. I felt as if my heart had just fallen out of my ass or something, but I knew what I told her next would be even more painful.

Not only was it going to hurt me but her as well. Somehow, I felt it was what she needed. Tough love and cold-hearted pain at least after what she put all of us through all these years. I heard her lies one too many times. I waited until she was done, wiped my face and told my mom I hated her and that I didn't ever want to see her again. I know I didn't mean it but at that time I did. From that day forward, I cut her off and started to enjoy life without her and with the people that were in it. The ones who never left and tried so hard to protect us.

My grandma was now mom to me. Although it was already like that in papers, it became super clear from that day, and I really started to feel it. As a child, every day was quite painful; not being able to wake up to my mom at any time of the day, not being able to spend time with her, getting our nails done, mall runs, even hair dates it all sucked. Teenage years came and I started to see that holidays sucked too without her as well as not being able to tell her about a certain boy I was crushing on or later on picking out dresses for homecoming and prom, all that good stuff.

Being in extra curriculum activities was probably the worst for me. I was really good in track but never had my parents there to support or see my success. It was normal for me to always go over to a friend/teammate's house and connect with their parents who were always involved. It gave me a sense of support through them and I'm forever grateful to them. Growing up without my mom was hard but it wasn't always bad. I was truly blessed to have my grandparents and other family members to help fill that void.

My grandma always made it happen, showed a lot of love, and did a very awesome job with us. In fact, the best day ever was the 2009 state championship. My grandfather was very ill and my grandma left his side for a couple of hours and came 4-5 hours away to Grand Rapids just to see me run. That may have been my best day ever. Over time, my mom called and tried to reach out. I didn't like to answer or always had a nasty attitude when forced to talk to her. She would try and visit too but we all refused to see her, and if she popped up, we just acted as if we didn't notice her.

By then she was forcing us to accept her, but it only continued to go downhill from there. I was completely done and refused to allow her to hurt me any more than she had already done or anyone else I cared about. My grandpa received his wings later in 2009 and that was when I finally saw my mom again without spinning her. My grandpa and I were the only few people my mom really connected to. While others called her a drug addict and judged her for her looks, parenting and whatever else they said about her, we tended to stay by her side, praying and loving her.

With me not talking to her and my grandpa gone, she ended up telling me she felt so alone. Hearing her vent to me still didn't ease any pain on my end. She ended up saying when she received the news that my grandpa was gone, she wanted to jump off the rehab building stating that she felt like nothing was left here for her anymore. Of course, it was a piece of upsetting news to hear how lost she became from losing her dad, but so lost as a person that she didn't even acknowledge her babies.

That somehow, we became that distant and we weren't even worth living for. She wanted to jump and didn't realize how affected we would be.

After my grandpa passed and my mom shared her feelings with me, everything between us started to fade. Now entering my young adult years, starting college and just trying to figure out life without her, it all kind of started to feel numb. I didn't care anymore if she wasn't coming back, and by then any type of faith I had went down the drain a while ago. I got the hang of being without her, and when I became a young mom which I had no clue at all what I was doing, I knew one thing for sure that I'd never ever leave my child no matter what. I wouldn't make the mistake of making him try and survive in this world alone without me. A couple of years went by, and in 2012 I had Justin. I thought that with all I had been through, he was the best thing that's ever happened to me.

I loved and felt so connected to him. He is my own flesh and I wouldn't leave even if I tried. A day or two after delivery unaware, I received a call and guess what? It was my mom. She congratulated me and said she was coming to visit her grandbaby. I ended the call with a hell no, she would not in any circumstances put my child through any hurt or pain that she did with me. My mom was like a mini gangster lol! So, she kept calling back threatening and hollering going back and forth with me that she was coming anyway no matter what.

I went on to say over my dead body. She will not be in my son's life, and if she was feeling froggy, Royal Oak police would be waiting at the door for her if she tried anything. I would have them escort her out and act as if I didn't know her at all. The thing is, I didn't feel an ounce of guilt or any sympathy towards her anymore. Now grown with a child, there was nothing she could teach or tell me. A couple of days later, I received another phone call and it was once again my mom. This time though she didn't want to argue, fuss or fight. Oddly, she just wanted to talk while I just listened.

That day my grandpa must have been shining down on us because something felt different. My mom apologized for the hundredth time, but this was a real sincere apology. She apologized about everything; not being in our lives and being the mom we needed and expected her to be. My mom really took accountability and explained her situation – the demons and sickness she constantly battled with while trying to make it out. She went on to say the last thing my grandpa said to her before he passed was, "Your kids, when you make it off these streets because you will, thank your kids. They really saved you. Not a day went by without them praying for you to come home. I know for a fact that God heard your children's prayers."

My mom ended by letting me know she would do whatever it took no matter the time to be in her grandchild's life, and to restore our relationship, she loved me and would see me soon. After that, I really didn't know what just happened, but I felt deep down in me that everything she said was genuine. I could somehow feel through the phone in her voice that she was tired of living that hard life on the streets, like her body was now overly tired of being constantly worked from fighting that street life.

She was finally ready to come home and piece together whatever life God had planned for her to live with her family. Finally, just finally, the day came in early 2013 and I can proudly say my mom got and stayed clean, and still is. At first, it started with getting our relationship back on track with a lot of talking and forgiving. Then, she finally met her grandson for the first time in the summer of 2013 when he was about seven or eight months old. I was ecstatic. Finally, after all this time I have my mom back. I was overjoyed to be able to celebrate my son's first birthday with my mom by my side helping and preparing for her grandson's party.

Since then, my mom hasn't missed a thing, that is until she moved. My mom and I restored our relationship and until this day she's my best friend but after repairing our relationship, my mom wanted a change in scenery and a chance to repair her relationship with my sister. My sister ended up moving to North Carolina after high school and she was first on our mom's list that is after me. My grandma became sick, so my mom stayed to help take care of her until she passed in 2018.

Although it was the beginning of a horrible year for me, I was supportive of my mom moving to grow a relationship with my sister. The trauma that was caused throughout my childhood prepared me for various things that I experienced at an early age. With raising my child, I was prepared to never miss anything that went on in his life. I am my kids' biggest supporter, I attend all events, games, conferences and whatever he's part of mama is there.

I loved every bit of having the second chance to parent my child the way I needed to be parented, no matter how weird that may sound. I got a chance to enjoy and create new moments with him instead of reflecting on the bad ones with my mom. In this part of my life, I was able to experience the understanding of forgiveness, address the pain, develop a forgiving mind through empathy, use other strengths to forgive and most importantly develop a forgiving heart. At the same time, I learned how to begin mastering parenthood through absent parents and repair a relationship someone couldn't dare break. I know pretty interesting right, but how can you ever share your experiences with others if you aren't ready to take that chance of forgiveness.

Second Time Around Notes

Who do you need to forgive and who are you ready to forgive?

_____

_____

_____

_____

_____

_____

_____

_____

_____

_____

_____

_____

_____

Double Up

Now y'all remembered I said I was a preacher's kid, and ain't nothing worse than being a pk kid and being pregnant. Not only are your parents/family members looking at you sideways but the church members as well. I couldn't catch a break. It's like the most annoying thing a person can ever do is judge you let alone your family, especially when you're trying to just figure out life itself. That's why this next version of me scared the living shit out of me not just because I wasn't ready but also because of the pressure I had on myself of not allowing people to judge me and what they thought was best for me instead of me knowing.

At this time in life, I was given the chance to be my best and favorite person to be a mom. Many women don't have the chance to experience motherhood due to a variety of reasons. The fact that I was given another, I took on that challenge without knowing what was to come. Motherhood definitely has its ups and downs, but I wouldn't trade it for anything. Of course, my overprotective grandma didn't want me to leave home to go and experience dorm life because of everything the sinful world had to offer she claimed.

Being hard-headed I went anyway but to a small local one called Marygrove College. I thought that would be better and it would be easier for her to say yes than going out of state, plus I was getting a scholarship for track there. So, the year was almost over, and I was living the life, so I thought with my own place (as we thought back then), no rules, and technically living with my boyfriend who I was just madly in love with. He was a junior at the time. Man, I was enjoying college life (some of y'all understand) and I was completely feeling myself, and nothing could stop the fun, so I thought.

As young adults, of course, there was plenty of fun and games and sad to say but intercourse. I mean it's college life and some of y'all were doing it earlier than that but that's another topic. All year went by and we were being protective and safe and yet we still ended up having a oops. I ended my first year of college pregnant and that was definitely the wrong news to bring home. So, I did what I thought was best at the time mainly because I was terrified of being responsible for another whole human being, scared of what people might think, especially my family.

I didn't want to lose my boyfriend and most of all, I didn't want to give up my life, at least the new free one outside of my grandma's death grip. I was eight weeks pregnant and ended up making the decision of having an abortion. I felt so embarrassed and low not just because I was a freshman and pregnant but because I knew better it was against my religion. We just didn't believe in killing life especially for really no reason at all and most of all letting my grandma be right. Back then during the abortion, no one knew. Just my roommate and my boyfriend, and now all of you guys.

During the process of aborting my baby, my boyfriend wasn't the supportive type that I needed at the time. Thinking about it now, I don't even really know what I needed and didn't want to complain to bring on any more problems to our situation. Until the following year, unfortunately God showed me clear as day what I needed. It was my amazing nine-year-old son that I have now. Yes, little miss sneaky pants met my knucklehead baby father and ended my second year of college very similar to my first, it was a double up. I know, I know the choices I had made were really childish, immature, and selfish back then.

Only this time I was very strong on not wanting an abortion. I took it as I shouldn't have been doing what I was doing that got me pregnant in the first place. I should have focused on my books or been somewhere running and trying to keep that scholarship of mine. I also felt so guilty about the first abortion that I thought this was my karma. The worst part is I was already about 15 weeks before I even knew I was pregnant basically finding out the sex. When I found out, I talked with my sister who never judges me or the decisions I make, and of course God and eventually my son's father. I ended up keeping the baby not because I wanted to keep my son's dad around (that's the first thing everyone assumes), but because of my guilt from the first abortion, and the pain I went through.

I had absolutely no idea what I was doing but promised myself I would never fall through with the decision of abortion again. This time around, I still didn't have the support at least like I wanted it to be from my son's dad, but I mean who would blame him at the time, we were still young, just figuring out what we really wanted to make of ourselves after college. At least he was, seeing it was his graduating year. On top of all of that, we had just ended things and he already had his heart set on another girl.

After all that decision making, I had a long talk with God, that if he guided me through this pregnancy and this next chapter of my life as a mom and made sure we were always good, I promised I would do my part as a mother and give this child the best life possible even if I had to do it alone being a single mom. From the day I had little J, I never broke that promise despite all the circumstances I faced and I never plan to no matter what life continues to throw at me.

If you think a guy can show you the best version of yourself, have a kid and it will change your whole mindset; it will literally change your whole life. Justin Jr has truly shown me that "being a mother is learning about strengths you didn't know you had, and dealing with fears you didn't know existed", (Linda Wooten). Being a mom, I have experienced a lot over the years and never let that or anything for that matter interfere with my duties as a mother. With my son's dad, while we tried to come together to raise a child, we went through our trials and had our differences constantly.

I have experienced heartbreak, which is normal with him, but also a case of domestic violence, kidnapping (some might call it) but I guess you can't technically take your own kid. Police visits, cps calls, plus so much more and of course the number one thing that's bound to happen at some point; drama, drama, and more drama between each other's family members, other baby mamas, and just outsiders in general. I swear I have been to family court so much I'm sure they know me on a first-name basis.

I'm not bashing my son's dad at all, but I went through hell that I brought upon myself and my child by being selfish, knowing that I wasn't cut for bringing life into such a broken situation. Just stating; to take all that and become the mom I am today is priceless and I don't regret it now that I look back at things. Now I'm not innocent either, I did my dirt. I mean who wouldn't want a family after a while or at least try to make one work? So I played my games, was jealous and very controlling at times.

Ultimately, I just wanted to give my child a bit of a better childhood than what I had. My parents didn't raise me; my grandparents did. My dad was never really there so by not allowing Big J to be a dad; I was bringing my son down that same path. I started to control parenting and only have it and look at things my way. Which if he didn't follow, I would at times hold our child against him and almost use him as a pawn. Although some might leave and never want to be bothered with the mess, he stayed and dealt with it and also penalized me for it as well.

It started to become a competition of who had the most control. Not realizing that when we brought our child into this world it was no longer about us and that was the hardest thing to learn years after our son was born. Along the way, I told myself I had to be a different person and change my ways. Over the years, I matured and let him be the parent he wanted to be instead of the parent I wanted him to be. Maturity is not by age, but by the acceptance of your responsibilities. I got another chance to learn how to let my son's dad be a father and for the first time, we became friends, started co-parenting like a normal family.

Now it's still not perfect and we still have our situations but the best part of it all is that we gave our son a chance to grow up with a peaceful mindset knowing that though his parents weren't together, they were giving him the best life possible as two mature adults should. I'd stop trying to be both mom and dad and just enjoy being his mom. I had promised God I would do whatever it took to be the best mom to that little boy and going through those trials and tests (because that's exactly what they were) was part of my adventure.

It's what makes me the mother I am now, and the woman I strive to become to show my son what to look forward to in marriage when he grows up. I always thought that if I could do things differently, it would be so much better but then I soon realized it was what I went through that changed me into this supermom and if I didn't go through what obviously was what I needed at the time, I wouldn't have the chance to tell young people to wait and enjoy life.

Having a child is exciting and all but it should definitely be at the right time at the right moment. With all the choices I've made – good or bad – they have shaped me into a pretty good co-parent, and independent woman I would say. God held up his end too as I knew he would, we have never been without even when I made some of the dumbest choices ever, he has always guided me to bigger and better things for my son, and us.

I might not have gotten everything I wanted but I was never without. Even when my faith, strength, and heart were tested numerous times, I still beat the odds. My child has never lacked anything. He definitely wants everything but hey what kid doesn't. We have always had support from family, friends, and other single moms/families, which I am so thankful for. Let me be the first to make it clear that nothing is wrong with getting help from others! We (collectively including myself) women of this age can be so prideful.

We act as if we don't need anything from anyone (not even the dad) when ultimately, we do. Simply picking your child up from school or daycare, taking them to that sports game or practice matters. I have the opportunity to meet just about all my son's school needs and functions because my job helps and allows me to, and also with the support of others. During the pandemic, I worked all the way through and was able to still perform my duties as a mom with help from others.

Even when it seems like it doesn't, small things of that nature go a very long way. Sad to say even the big talk "Child Support" that's been an issue recently definitely helps at some point no matter the amount. I know we moms say we don't need it, but help comes in all shapes and forms and it still helps. Take the help, it doesn't make you less of a mother or woman at all. There's no one more independent than a single woman raising a child period! But with help, I like to think of it as God sending different ones as a blessing into my life – our lives.

I also felt that if ever anything was to happen to me, I knew Justin was covered with tons of love, prayers, and support. There are other women out there who may have gone through the same thing or worse, and when the time is right, they will see and experience their own growth in motherhood and themselves. If you are in this kind of situation, then I am here to let you know that you're not alone and I promise it will get better; just keep pushing. Sharon Jaynes wrote;

"Successful mothers are not the ones that never struggled, they are the ones that never give up despite the struggles."

Being given the opportunity of having another child has taught me so much more about myself again that I didn't even know existed. I had no idea the hardships that I and potentially my child might have had to face – finishing school, working, weekly groceries, sitters, etc. But giving up was simply not an option for me. It's only when you take responsibility for your life that you truly discover how powerful you really are.

I can't express enough how much all these different life experiences throughout this book have molded me into the woman I am, but parenting has done so much more mentally. As parents, we fail, we try harder and sometimes we still fail. But we don't quit and we never give up. Yes, our children can see our flaws but like my son, he has shown me that I am enough and that I am a human who's bound to make mistakes. Motherhood has truly made me a better person; it was something I had to go through in order to grow. It gave me life, by creating life. For the second time around, I have endured that I am more than just a mom.

Second Time Around Notes

Who are you and what defines you?

_____

_____

_____

_____

_____

_____

_____

_____

_____

_____

_____

_____

GAP

At some point in your life, you will find a gap as if life has failed you and slipped off the tracks for a moment. I'm sure we've all been there at a point where a piece is missing. Like what noun? No, I spelled it right what am I going to do without this person, place or thing? How can I fill this gap? There are some lucky ones out there that may not have experienced this ride but I'm sure everyone has had the pleasure of second chances on love a couple of times to be honest. Yes, if I have kept you interested enough this far, then you've reached a good part.

I've given my biggest second chances in life to a handful of lames. But there's always that one person you can't seem to leave. That one person you just have to be toxic with because you are. Don't be offended. I was toxic too at a point. No matter what a guy did and how many times he did it, I had every excuse in the book to cover up the messed-up shit that I gave countless chances to. I've given plenty of chances to the wrong men and I've done nothing but either learn from it or make the same damn dumb mistake again, then after that, it stops being a mistake and turns into a choice.

I'm sure you all think this next chapter is probably about the father of my child but there's not enough ink in the world (kidding) but this chapter is called GAP and this person filled exactly that – a GAP. Who would have thought that trying to make an ex jealous in the club would lead me to one of the hardest things in life and a tough choice that I don't regret making, opening up my heart and mind again?

Of course, everything was all good and gravy in the beginning then boom all hell breaks loose. I'm joking. It's not exactly like that but eventually, the problems and issues would come. So, we either deal with them or not. But interestingly, nine times out of ten, as humans we were dealing with them at least at some point until we've had enough. So, with this new guy, within two years, some things were quite a smooth ride at least for the majority of the route.

Then like cars, we hit a couple of bumps, potholes and dodged some ditches, but I continued the ride no matter how many tires were still left on. If you're lucky enough you will survive it all and eventually get to your destination. Well unfortunately for me, I made a pit stop. After a couple of years, we came to an end and the ride was over. But just within that time frame I literally became the best adult version of myself with this individual. I learned things I never really kind of cared about in life or thought of caring about until I met him, especially at my age.

Not because I didn't want to learn but a lot of them were things I didn't know because I was being shielded from them, spoiled, or over-protected while growing up and even in my adult age. And when I actually grew up and started doing well for myself, I gave it all up in 2018 when my grandma passed. This was very simple stuff though like not stressing over what people might think about you and don't give a "f" just do you.

Live life but not too comfortable where I'm stuck living paycheck to paycheck; invest, save at least five to ten thousand or more, just general life lessons we should all know. And to me, the most important thing was being happy again and finding who Kylia once was as a person.

At that time, I wasn't going after my goals or even living up to my full potential. I was not being smart with money, instead, I was just spending it recklessly. My credit score was in the 500s and I didn't have my own place with a child. I had simply given up on life altogether and it was quite embarrassing. I just knew that man was thinking sweetie bye "go get yourself together," instead of worrying about liking someone. Instead, Deon (I know y'all were waiting for a name) wanted me to want more for myself and more out of life than just living day-to-day with no purpose, no fun, no laughter, no meaning.

On our first date, he wasn't even trying to get in my draws but kept asking what my credit score was, if I had savings, credit cards, and just being a smart gentleman. He understood very clearly that I'd lost someone very special, but he was like so what? They passed, they aren't here anymore so what are you going to do with your life now? Sit around and pout about it? Just continue to give up? Keep praying that God sends them back? Pretty harsh right?

I know I thought the same thing but at the same time, it was also exactly what I needed to hear to get out of my funk. Deon had saved me from what was one of the darkest places that I would never ever want to experience again and hope no one else does. 1 was losing myself, losing the mother character I fought so hard to become/create, and just starting to fail at life in general because I was mad that God took away the one person I felt I could never see leave me.

I lost everything and had two cents to my name basically, but he didn't judge me. Instead, he showed me the way out of that dark hole. He showed me how to live successfully through discipline, proper preparation, confidence, fun and love. He wanted to help me get there or at least show me where to even start. I know you're wondering where's the second chance I gave him. Unfortunately, after this great time I spent with Deon, he wasn't ready for the next step when I was. Instead, he broke my poor little heart and I'm female so you know I was super dramatic and extra about it.

I was pissed like all this growing I've done, opening myself up to life again, to a new person that I thought so highly of and it wasn't for him. I was so over it. We had a big argument about it, and we ended. Deon was the first person that did a little better than the last which caused me to assume and make stuff what really wasn't maybe more than what it really was. I was a little vulnerable.

Now he wasn't a saint either; he did his dirt too and showed actions of wanting more but said otherwise which was very confusing. You know how guys play that role nowadays. I can't complain though because I allowed it and stuck with it for so long. A couple of months went by and we hadn't talked, then I did something I thought I could never see myself doing because my pride was in control. I wrote down all the pros and cons of being with this man and just having him in my life. Well, the good outweighed the bad.

So, I did what smart people do every now and then for that special person we don't want to lose. I gave in and gave another chance at allowing this man back into my life but of course differently this time. I know what y'all thinking second chance at what? He already stated he didn't want to be together. But he was so damn charming and very good at convincing and having me believe certain things he said that made me think it would be different. I truly felt I could not live without this man.

Praying that if another chance came by again, I would try my best to make this work even if I had to change myself for him to commit. We definitely started back off as friends as if somewhere down the line we must have missed a step or two. Yea that same man who had me crying at night when the kid was asleep, the one that had me teary-eyed when that one pandora song hit the radio, yes that guy, I took him back. Also, this was the guy who taught me more about life lessons than certain family members and close friends.

Someone who not just wanted relations with me but wanted to help me succeed in life whether we made it as a couple, friends, or enemies, and for that I am forever grateful. Oh, but it absolutely didn't work, and no we were not together till this day. I know, I know what you all are thinking d.u.m.m.y I mean at the time shoot me too, I thought the same thing, like not again, WTF! Then it hit me when I realized the bigger picture. In order to love who you are, you cannot hate the experiences that shaped you.

The number of lessons I began to learn and take away just from this situation alone was priceless. For one, never let a man show you twice that he doesn't want you, which absolutely stung like a bee because ain't no one trying to hear that at all. Especially when you put time and effort into such a meaningful situation. I started to be mad at myself because I changed more of myself for someone who didn't even ask me to, trying to be someone I wasn't.

I was mad at myself for not knowing my worth and valuing myself. Never let someone have so much control over you that you change being yourself for them or try your best to please them. Know who you are, know what you want, know what you deserve and don't settle for less. I looked back at how far I had come, took accountability, and begin to work on loving me. I didn't do what most people would do – pointing fingers, complaining about who did what to each other when still nothing was going to change after all that blaming.

"The Truth is everyone is going to hurt you. You just have to find the ones worth suffering for" (**Bob Marley**).

Tough times only make you stronger and I realized that the right person will make you fall in love with yourself too. I left that "situationship" (as they call it these days) knowing who Kylia was the moment the same cycle continued. I said no and as bad as I wanted to keep giving this man all of me, I found my voice. I spoke up when things weren't right or seemed fair, I wasn't a yes wo(man) anymore, and that even helped me in other situations as well regarding friends, jobs, and certain family members.

Though we weren't together, in the long run, I took a risk and came out with a double win. I experienced heartbreak but also how to heal correctly in my own way from it without all the drama because we are still good friends as of today. Face it; nowadays we are willing to kill each other because we can't have a certain person or because our feelings get a bit bruised. Through my experience, you can love one person romantically but still have an open mind.

I also took away self-care by addressing my own problems, removing toxic energy, and holding myself accountable for things I did or said that stuck with me in the long run for other situations. I learned that even if that person is dead or alive, life goes on regardless and you can go on to live your life peacefully without them and even cherish amazing memorable moments once shared. I started to do whatever was best for Kylia and have no fear, concerns or even feel a bit guilty about it.

Overall, I learned how to open my heart and believe again even after him. I've had the opportunity of allowing someone to love me properly and for once I accepted it, even after Deon and others which I thought would never happen. As of today, I am now in a safe, happy, loving relationship and in somewhat thanks to Deon, not necessarily to him personally but the situation. I noticed I had a hard time believing but had a lot of good things around me like family, friends and love. All those things were worth believing in or simply worth giving a second go-round.

In life just because you know what you want doesn't mean you'll always get it. Sometimes we meet people that last forever or last enough for us to just live in the moment with. Every moment is your moment so make it count. I lived my moment, have you?

Second Time Around Notes

Are you living your best life and are you making it count?

_____

_____

_____

_____

_____

_____

_____

_____

_____

_____

_____

_____

_____

Second Time Around

Depending on your character, you have people who are forever giving out second chances. People who have learned their lesson the first time, and don't think twice about giving anything or anyone another chance ever again. Then people like me who have always had a heart so big that I continued to give people countless chances and the benefit of doubt. Do you ever feel like you give too much and never ask for anything in return?

I give out a million do-overs for some reason. I always felt like I would feel guilty if I didn't give others the fairness of another chance at least to reevaluate themselves realizing that it wasn't up to me for making them see another opportunity; it was within them to take it. I feel like you can find the good in everyone, and that's probably why I end up in the most difficult situations that continue to occur in my life. I believe that everything happens for a reason.

I will continue to take risks, chances, and opportunities because that's what makes me who I am. That's what made me take the chance at writing this book. The truth is people get so caught up in thinking they have forever when we never really know when our time will end. After all that you'll experience in life, if there's a little bit of a second time around to make the second experience even doper than the first, why hesitate? Live life to the fullest as people would say. I know I would because if I didn't, I knew I would always be wondering or be thinking of all these what-ifs and should have's which will eat my brain away.

And I'd rather it be an oops than a what if. Because truth be told, in the end, we only regret the chances we didn't take, relationships we were afraid to have, and the decisions we waited too long to make. Maya Angelou said;

"I did then what I knew how to do. Now that I know better, I do better."

I'm not saying you should follow my steps, don't be a dummy. I was a mess and sometimes still is but realize that it's within yourself to make these decisions to be the best version of you. Sometimes you got to dig a little deeper to figure out if that job, that knucklehead boy, that family member, that certain religion or whatever it is that you're debating right now about needs a second chance or if it's worth it.

I'm not saying that you should take every chance given either. Let's not be stupid; life will forever be disappointing. But if offered another chance at something you feel you may have taken for granted or willing to learn from previous failure, take it. Why wait? Don't do it to please anyone but yourself. Do it for you to be at peace, and for you to be better in life. Everyone is always saying you only live once but have you thought about an experience or opportunity that has already passed and you get another chance to relive it or remake?

Why not make that only life you have to live even better? The key lesson I tend to take away from this resourceful life is what's meant for me will eventually come back around. So it's up to me to decide from there. Just get back up when life knocks you down because it's going to continue to come back. I'm sure some of you thought this book would probably be about me being madly in love with a guy that I gave a second chance one too many times.

Nope, I wanted to help others look at life differently through every experience, opportunity, twist or turn that I was given throughout this life journey. If you didn't take anything away from this book, here's an opportunity to try again and make things right the second time around.

Second Time Around Notes

Are you ready for the Second Time Around?

_____

_____

_____

_____

_____

_____

_____

_____

_____

_____

_____

_____

_____

About the Bio

Kylia is a single mom from Detroit working in the administration field. Being the sole provider for her child working hard determined to be something not only to herself but also her child. She's able to do something inspiring and enjoyable. Live life and write about it. Writing has always been important to Kylia. From a young age writing down her

thoughts, prayers, feelings were just her normal outlet, a since of relief but grew to become the beginning of so much more. Writing has always been her happy place, where Kylia could release her thoughts and expand her imagination. Back in high school was when Kylia started to really put pen to paper and realize this was what she was good at. It would simply start by expressing her feelings about her first love, activities she was in, and just everyday life situations. While growing up, and away from her mom Kylia would write how she felt about the trauma caused by her parents. While writing these daily journal entries' one Sunday Kylia was prophesied, she would be an author. The prophet said, "she was destined to write and she would publish multiple books. For majority of her career Kylia pursued childcare as her path to follow putting a pause on writing. When her grandma got sick, she started back writing and taking her prayers she prayed for her grandma to paper. With Kylia's grandma passing in 2018 and switching careers to administration coping with her grandmas passing she begin to follow her heart deciding to focus and purse what gives her life again. She published her first book in 2022 and its only the beginning of so much more in store and to come.

Contact Kylia @: kyliabillups@yahoo.com

Interested In Writing and/or Publishing a Book?

Visit Dr. Synovia @a2zbookspulishing.net